Beauty In HEALING

a collection of poetry & prose

Also by B. Vigil

Beauty In Darkness

Anthologies B. Vigil is featured:

Shadow of the Soul

As Darkness Falls

Love Is Helpless

A Touch of Temptation

Don't Forget Him

Silent Tears of a Woman

Ukraine: The Night and the Fire

Beauty In HEALING

a collection of poetry & prose

B. VIGIL

300 SOUTH MEDIA GROUP
NEW YORK

This book is presented as a collection.

BEAUTY IN HEALING

ISBN-13: 978-1-957596-25-9 (paperback)
ISBN-13: 978-1-957596-26-6 (ebook)

Published by 300 South Media Group

I would like to dedicate this book to my daughters.

Life can be a crazy and cruel thing and knowing that I can't save you from heartbreak in the future or from any pain you may experience as you girls get older; may my words ALWAYS be a guiding light for you. A gentle reminder that you can heal yourself from all of it, even when it feels like you don't have the strength to carry through it.

May you always remember that you have my blood pumping through your veins, and with it, you ALSO have my strength. I love you girls to the moon and forward.

TABLE of CONTENTS

Thank you for the tragedy.
I need it for my art.

—Kurt Cobain

Getting To This Point

It all happened so fast: the start, the tragedy, the end. I'm not sure at what point inside of me it all changed. I was in such a deep place of complacency. I knew that I couldn't live like that any longer. The void. The abandonment. The feeling of being alone, even when I wasn't. I saw so much of it growing up, and no matter how much I swore it would never be me, I found myself in similar situations.

I came to the conclusion that the root of most of my problems was unhealed trauma from both my childhood and as an adult. At the time, I had toxic traits that I wouldn't acknowledge. I kept creating this codependency on others like my life depended on it, and at that time in my life, it did. I was at a place in life where I wasn't whole by myself.

I hadn't figured out who I was or who I needed to be yet. Over time, my eyes opened slowly. I wasn't living in this illusion that I wouldn't be complete without someone else by my side. And unfortunately, like most, I had to learn all of it the hard way. It took putting my all into a person and having them completely sabotage our relationship and ruin everything that we built to learn that. And let me tell you something: when you do that to yourself, and they leave, you are ultimately left with nothing, or at least that's how it feels. You feel like you are a shell of the person you were before them. All you will have at that point is nothing but a mirror standing in front of you, asking yourself how you even got to this point in the first place.

I've learned that not only is self-love one of the hardest things in life to achieve, but so is self-accountability. Especially when all you have known or done is self-sabotage because you didn't know any better and you were afraid.

All due to the fact you were hurt and trying to navigate through life after, with no one to guide you the right way through your trauma. I was always the over-achiever, the over-thinker, the over-lover. I was the one who used to think that I had to pour into every single cup around me to feel whole. To be whole. It truly is just like the saying, "*You can only pour so much because you can't pour from an empty cup.*"

And my God, did I learn that the hard way. Painfully.

Self-awareness came first. Learning who I was at the time, my bad habits and toxic traits, and learning to see the light shining out from inside of my chest, even as I sat in the darkest moments of my life.

Self-realization was next. It was a series of moments deciding what I wanted and who I wanted to be. Then, I realized just how much work I was going to have to put in to make it all happen.

Self-acceptance came after that. It took dealing with demons and acknowledging situations and events in my life that I was in denial about. It was accepting everything that had happened up until this point. I had to acknowledge even the darkest parts of my soul, which also meant forgiving myself and everyone around me. Little did I know this was just the beginning of all of it, too.

Next was layer after layer of change, more internally than not. It started with learning to be both positive and to think positively no matter how hard it felt, and this was a hard step for me. I tend to be pessimistic at times due to things I've experienced and applying it to everyday situations that arise. I tend to think the worst of every situation and person; I had very little hope left in me at that point in time. This was huge. I taught myself how to look up again. I had to do deep, uncomfortable, hard shadow work.

I had to ask myself, "Why am I the way I am? How can I become better?"

It was changing mindsets.
Perspectives.
Beliefs.
Habits.
Routines.

It's telling yourself that you're better than what you've been doing to yourself, and more importantly, it's **BELIEVING** it.

After all of that, which is **A LOT**, comes self-love.

Self-love is one of the hardest battles we face as humans, for the mere fact that most of us tend to base our worth on how we are treated by others, which leads to a road where we end up treating ourselves worse, both consciously and subconsciously.

Over time, we become our own harshest critics, which can be even worse if we've never been loved correctly.

Our minds become our worst enemy. Our nemesis. Emotions are misplaced and misunderstood. For this reason, it is one of the hardest things to do for ourselves. We not only have to tell ourselves that we are **WORTHY** of healthy love, peace, and stability, but we also have to **BELIEVE** it.

How many happy faces do you know that are carrying broken souls that show through their eyes because they do not know how to believe it or are afraid of it? How many times in your life do you remember begging for mercy, even if it's just for a night, from your own mind? We have to learn to love the thunderstorms in our souls. We have to learn to love the sun when our hearts are starting fires in the desert. We have to love ourselves on the days when we feel like we can't get out of bed. We have to love ourselves on the days when you feel like you're too much for the people around you.

We have to learn to love ourselves even when we feel like we cannot bear what is standing in front of us with our own reflection in the mirror. We must learn empathy, compassion, love, and understanding. This doesn't just go for others. We also need to learn this for ourselves. And do you want to know the crazy part after all of that?

Self-love isn't where the healing journey ends, either. After walking through and working on all of that, next is self-accountability. You see clearer, which means you know better now. In turn, now you have to become better. You also have to work twice as hard to stay there after. You have to fight yourself internally and resist those around you externally so as to not go back to old habits, old ways, previous relationships, or old places of comfort. It's sometimes a lot of back and forth until we figure it out and learn it for ourselves, and if you're anything like me, you've had to learn that the hard way, too.

One of the hardest things for me to accept was learning that we become different people after trauma in more ways than one.

We see life different
we love different,
speak different,
and move different.

Even more so when we start the healing journey. Once we open those doors, there's really no going back to the person we were before. We may find ourselves going back to old habits or people, but it's never with the same eyes.

And let's be honest, most people do fall back into it. We go back to old places of comfort, even if they currently bring you more pain. It's a war between your head and your heart and a never-ending one at that.

A war that leaves us feeling worse about ourselves after every time we catch ourselves going back to it. We are more conscious at this point, so even as we do it, we know the outcomes before they happen. We see the train wreck ahead waiting for us, and we still act shocked after it happens. Now, we have to work twice as hard to get back up; we will eventually learn over time that the back and forth is just a means to keep us down and serves us no purpose.

This is the stage where we finally see the truth, where we finally see that we have outgrown this environment and that it's time to finally let go.

It's a ton of work. It's a mountain full of obstacles. Some people don't make it out alive. Sometimes, the weight of it all becomes overbearing. Whether it's trauma or the pain of healing, I get it. I've been there before. I've been on both sides of it.

Sometimes, just sometimes, it's easier to just go back to what we know. We go back to what feels like home and just stay strong where we are, even if the place we call home is hell.

But let me tell you something from making it out to the other side:

You owe yourself so much more than what you're allowing yourself to go through. If you hold on and fight just a little bit longer, eventually, it stops becoming a fight. Over time, it just becomes muscle memory, even for your heart.

You will have to allow yourself to mourn your old self. You will need to grieve for that part of your soul that was broken. You will, at some point, accept that there is no going back to the person you were before your trauma. So many of us focus so hard on going back to who we used to be, and healing was never meant to be about that.

Healing is about breaking your cocoon and growing into something more beautiful, something you never even realized you could become. You have to just believe. You will become stronger, wiser, more resourceful, more passionate, and more aware of your emotions. You will learn not to react to your emotions anymore and learn the power that comes with being in control of them. The old you had so much to learn still.

The old you didn't know how to move to dodge bullets, didn't know how to read people's intentions and didn't know how to love yourself, but one day you will figure all of it out.

I write this as a map, in no particular order, that these healing pieces will come in for you. Everyone who heals deep trauma goes through this in one way or another.

It will come on a sunny afternoon when you feel like there's no hope. It will come with the glistening of the moon reflecting off of the tears rolling down your face.

You will smile and acknowledge it and say, *"There you are. I knew you were still there."* And before you know it, it will grow from being a little flicker in your eyes to a light that is just pouring out of your soul.

Can I tell you a secret?

It's not a light at the end of the tunnel like we were all told to expect growing up. It's a light that illuminates from inside of you. It is not ahead of you. It is **WITHIN** you. You will see that there is hope. You are the hope. I stand here before you on the other side of healing to tell you that it is beautiful here. The sun shines a little brighter. The light becomes more beautiful than blinding to your eyes.

You learn to have such a deep passion for the darkness because you know you need to venture both through it and out of it to be where you are today. You empathize with everyone still in it because you remember, at one point, it was you. You start living again, not just surviving. I am standing here today to ask you to just hold on a little bit longer.

No matter what part of the journey you are on, I'm here to remind you that everything you need to get to where you're going in life is inside of you. You are the magic. You've always had it in you. And if you forget any of it on the hard days, I'll be right here through my words **ETERNALLY** to remind you of what you are capable of.

All or Nothing

My soul has always been such a reckless thing, especially when it comes to love.

I don’t know how to do anything in halves.

It's always been all or nothing. It has always been black and white for people like me.

Putting That Past to Rest

Letting go of you hurt,
but it doesn’t hurt nearly as much
as learning to let go
of the part of myself
that loved you.

Lost Boys

I used to be a naïve girl. I used to think that if I left doors unlocked and my lights on, that you'd make your way back home. The same way that Peter Pan always returned to Wendy's window. I used to think that if I loved the Beast you had become, that the prince in you would somehow return and find your way back to our love.

Reality eventually sank in with every day that passed. I had to learn the hard way that sometimes 'Lost Boys' are just that: lost boys. I had to learn that the people who become 'Beasts' by choice remain just that, beasts. I had to learn the art of loving unconditionally and then, immediately after, the art of letting go. I had to learn the hard way that people aren't always who they pretend to be or even what they show.

Before The Ruins

I used to believe in the saying, "You get what you give out to this world." I truly used to believe this. I based my whole persona on it, trying to bring love and light into everyone and everything in my life. Hoping for a chance of tasting it reciprocated.

But it's been far from equal in the life I've lived. Even when I move with pure intentions, especially when I love the most, I somehow always end up more broken than before. The love I have bestowed has never come back. I have never not once felt that love that I have given out.

Sometimes, the world is far more cruel than we could ever be.

Maybe that's why they call life a beautiful tragedy.

One day, I woke up,
and it didn't hurt anymore.

Dear Diary

Dear Diary,

I just want the pain to stop.
I've endured enough chaos for one lifetime.

I'm ready for stillness.
I'm ready to learn how to breathe
without having to be prepared for another war.

I'm ready for calmness.
I'm ready for peace.
I'm ready for more.

We Must Learn

Heal, and I say this heavily.
Because people really walk this earth
with the filter of their trauma
over their eyes,
and often destroy the best things for them.

Apologies Do Nothing

I used to always tell myself
that all I needed to let go
was an apology.

Until I realized that apologies
don't make the pain go away either.

Thank You

I thank the universe for your role in my life.
I thank you for the lessons I learned from our tragic love.
I thank you for cracking this heart open in a way that I never knew was possible.
Shattering it open to love you,
and now shattering it to let me go
Both will make me a better person in the future.

I never knew how much love I was capable of giving
until I loved you.

Graceful Girl

Females like her are a different breed.
They live by a code of gentleness and loyalty,
not necessarily just love.

Trials and tribulations have shown
her just how shaky the world can be,
in the name of it.

Promises have merely become words.
Plans are nothing more than dates with a ghost.
She allows everything to flow without resistance.
As gracefully as she lets things in,
she also lets them go.

More Than A Goddess

She loved harder than Aphrodite
Shined brighter than Artemis,

Stronger than Hera
More beautiful than Persephone

Wiser than Athena
More graceful than Hecate
And darker than Nyx.

You can't break a soul like hers.
Her purpose was ALWAYS greater than you.

Costly Decisions

Causing other people pain
just because they caused you pain,
doesn't bring you peace.

It only makes you one of **T H E M**.

Wide Awake

If you truly knew or understood
Just how precious your time is here,
You'd never let anything
pull you out of your peace.

Perception and Reality

If you look at me and all you see is darkness,
you don't know me at all.

People only see or point out flaws and insecurities
that they have within themselves;
whether they are acknowledged or not.

Every single one of us
carries both light and dark within

What you choose to see in me,
tells me everything I need to know about you.

Starry Eyes

There's always light to see in the dark;
you just have to adjust your eyes to it.

Just like the stars,
you'll never truly know
how bright and beautiful they are,
until you sit under them
in the darkest of skies.

No Loss

Both of what's meant for me and the one who really loves me wouldn't do anything in the world to hurt me. They won't leave. Ever. No matter how dark life gets, no matter what the road ahead of us looks like. The one that I'm waiting for is the one who holds my hand tighter before our biggest battles, reminding me that I'm not in this alone.

I never wanted makeshift. I never wanted a lover who ran away when life got tough. I never wanted anything temporary anyway. I am not interested in anyone who wants pieces of my soul and the love within my heart if their intention is just to leave anyway.

My Curse

I can't hate,
and I think that's what kills me the most.

I can't even hate
the ones who deserve nothing but my fury.

My heart is not capable of it anymore.

Even with every ounce of pain
that's been bestowed upon me,

I still find myself sitting here
wishing them nothing but the best.

It's a Process

Sometimes, some days, the weight of it all can become overbearing. It will hit you like waves crashing in, and it will cripple your ability to even breathe. Somedays, the noise on the inside will be louder than the noise around you. Some days will feel dark, no matter how bright the sun is around you. Somedays feel never-ending, and something as simple as taking life hour by hour feels like an eternity. There is no healing without these days.

The balance in life is just as brutal as it is beautiful. You have to have mercy on your heart during these times because the world around us and the world within us are storming at the same time sometimes. The one we need to be the kindest to in those moments isn't to anyone but ourselves. Tomorrow is another day.

Depths

Don't stare into my eyes too long, baby,
the pain that I hold in there
might break you too.

Worth the Price?

The hopeless romantic in me
almost cost me my soul,
more times than I can count.

My heart has always had trouble
accepting what my head already knew.

Closure

"Some endings don't get proper goodbyes."

But baby, them letting go and walking away,
was your closure.

You deserve so much more than that.
You deserve a love without question.
A love without conditions.

You deserve to be chosen.
I hope you never forget that.

Learning To Let Go

Oh, the stories these walls in the chambers of my heart could tell of laughter, happiness, and hope. Where it's now empty with memories was once lit up in the most beautiful ways. Filled with your love.

It may be vacant now, but it still echoes with your voice in here still. The promises of forever. The love that poured out ferociously between us. My heart may not be what it once was anymore, but it's still worth loving--in need of some renovation and nothing less. She's still standing. Decaying yet beautiful. Echoing and yearning for the hope of tomorrow.

It's Far From Over

Healing is a lifelong journey.
Your battle doesn't stop just because the trauma does.
That's usually where it all begins.
The extreme highs and extreme lows.
The "what ifs" and "I need to knows."
All of the uncertainty and the loud noise of fear,
but if you listen closely,
you will hear a whisper of hope.
A whisper of love.
The whisper of better things coming;
better than you could ever dream of.

Two Choices

One of the hardest lessons you will ever learn in life,
is that not everyone wants to be saved.

Some people are so content in their own chaos,
no amount of love or life you give them,
will ever fix them.
For the simple fact of they don't want to change.

Some people's only identity is their tragedy.

In the end, we are faced with two choices:
Just love them or let them go.

Learning On My Own

My darkest nights weren't overcome
by searching for the sun.
Some days, it never came.
My worst days were survived by learning
how to navigate in those dark waters,
and learning how to become
my own light when I was lost.

And let me tell you a secret:
once you figure that out,
no one can ever steal that from you again.
It wasn't given, it was earned.
And it's yours to navigate through
anything your soul ventures through after.

Looking Into My Eyes

The person I used to be
can never come back,
I won't let her.
She was naïve.
She let her emotions dictate her life.
She was explosive and reckless.
She did the best she could, though,
and I'll forever respect her for that.
But this new person I have become,
came at a price that there are no refunds for:

Unimaginable loss
Tragedy
Pain

The lessons that I had to learn
burned the old me alive.
With no guidance or survival guide,
the only thing left to do was transform.

It feels like a whole lifetime has passed,
a whole different time and place.
But if you look deep enough into my eyes,
you can still see her weeping face.

Should Be Here, But You're Not.

I made it through another day without you.
Another month.
Another year.

And with everything good and bad that's come since,
I can't help but think about
how you were supposed to be here
for **A L L** of it.

Always

Of course, they are drawn to you, my dear.
You are a light.

And the light
always pulls out the most
questionable creatures from the dark.

Bleeding Art

When dealing with artists of any kind,
there's only one thing to watch for
when it comes to them

Pay attention to the art,
they bleed differently.

It Takes Time

Do you want to know why it hurt so much?
Because to you, it was real.
The love.
The connection.
The comfort.

Even if it wasn't a fairytale,
The feelings that **YOU** felt were real.

It's going to take some time to heal from that.

Be gentle with yourself.

Acceptance

It's okay, Baby,
You can tell the world I was the one who broke us.
You can tell them I was the monster.

But deep down, you know
every ounce of love that I had for you.

First, We Must Crumble.

There is nothing beautiful about being broken. We only say that to get through it. To try to be optimistic, But in reality, it's messy. It's pain with every breath you take. It's struggling to make it through the night because you feel like you're never going to be good enough.

It's everyone always leaving, even the ones who say that they won't.

And then it's you, pushing the good people away because you don't know what real love is, and you self-sabotage everything good subconsciously. It's waking up and faking it through the day.

It's smiling so much your face hurts around other people, only to go home and be numb after the day ends.

It's not being able to tell your friends what is going on anymore because you feel like an idiot at this point.

It's shutting down completely. It's numbing yourself to survive. It's hoping that one day someone will see through it all enough to care to pick up the pieces and still love you anyway.

And then it's the hope, it's always the fucking hope that kills us.

Betrayal

I think of all the tragedy I've gone through in life; the most painful of all came from betrayal.

It can come from anyone, anywhere, at any time. Often times without warning. Without a single drop of remorse or mercy on your heart.

The most painful ones come from those closest to you, be it family, friends, or lovers. It teaches us valuable life lessons, though.

It shows us that the only one who could ever truly have our backs and look out for us is ourselves. This was my hardest lesson.

I had to learn that everyone else in this world somehow seemed to only be out for themselves.

I learned at a young age that not everyone in this world has a heart like mine. Not everyone sees life as I do. Not everyone has a moral compass.

No matter the reasons behind any of it, we must learn to move on despite it.

We must find a way to carry on without any of it: without them, without closure, and without apologies. How we react to all of it becomes our karma.

We have to trust the universe enough to allow them to move as they must.

People who know your heart and choose to hurt you anyway, *don't deserve your love.*

We must learn to accept this.

They Say

They say in order to love someone else, you must first love yourself. I don't know about you, but it was always the opposite for me. For years, I found myself clinging to my lovers. I loved with such depth and intensity long before I even understood what it meant to love myself.

I didn't know the difference back then. And let me tell you something: when it came to him, anything was on the table. I would have done anything to please that man, and I did. It wasn't until years after he left, and we fell out that I learned what loving myself meant.

While I was in it, though? My love for him consumed me. I had never loved a human being more in my life. In my eyes, he was my hero. My protector.

He was the reason I wanted to fight for my life, the reason I wanted to become a better person, and the reason I started chasing my dreams. He inspired all of that in me when I didn't even know I had the drive to do it myself. That was the beauty in the beast of our story.

He helped me see parts of myself that I didn't even know existed or that I was capable of. He helped me learn how to love myself. He softened my edges. He taught me how to forgive myself. And ultimately, he taught me the art of unconditional love, and in our tragic ending, he taught me the art of letting go.

In the beginning, I did it all. My love was so pure for him, so you can imagine the demise that spiraled in its place when he left. I had to learn how to love myself first before I learned peace in letting go. I had to teach myself that not everyone deserves that kind of love.

It was on me the whole time to change the locks to my heart. I had to completely crumble and fall apart to retreat back to who I was before I knew he existed. **Except this time, I was coming back even better.**

More mature. With eyes wide open and a heart that was trying to bleed out all of the poison left inside, and the whole time, he was telling me that it was love.

I know better now. I see it as clear as black and white when someone's intentions don't match my own.

I only want real. I've only ever wanted real.

My life story and love stories are tragic reminders that not everyone has the same heart as you.

I'm just here to remind you that sometimes, just sometimes, loving someone else in the absence of yourself first doesn't make you any less strong. It just shows that you are more capable of it.

Sometimes, it just takes someone else to help us see it. And when you figure all of it out, you will become an unstoppable force of nature. You will heal in ways you couldn't comprehend before.

All of it is okay as long as you find your way back home to yourself in the end. Everything else can be handled. Everything is going to be okay.

Just like the quote from Caroline Forbes on TVD, "*Anyone capable of love is capable of being saved.*"

And I know someone else out there needed to hear that.

Self-Taught

I taught myself how to let go when I learned that the empty spaces were safer than the ones that carried chaos. Our tragic love made me realize that being alone is better than having something that's only half there. The lonely nights taught me that I don't need your arms to calm me down if nothing happened that required me to recover from.

The internal war inside of me taught me that, most times, my head was always right. It taught me not to always lead with my heart, but of course, she never surrenders without a fight.

Your love taught me that if things seem too good to be true, they usually are. And ironically, what taught me the most was the scars.

Fire Soul

People underestimate me.
Life has shown me
how to start my own flames,
burning brighter than anything
that can ever come *near me.*

Pure Intentions

I wear my heart on my sleeve
and love with everything I have.
Because if it all blows up,
I can rest knowing
it wasn't because anything fell through on my end.

Let Go

I'm not going to be that girl anymore.
I did enough.
I am enough.
I can let go now.

No matter how much it hurts.
No matter the scars it burns.

My story must go on.

Lessons

The waves taught me
that giving up was never a choice.

The flames of life taught me
how to use my own voice.

To get where we want in life,
sometimes we have to do things
we never thought we would.

The pain taught me lessons,
that no sunny days ever could.

Time has always shown
the true colors of familiar faces.

The darkness taught me
how to look for the light,
even in the most unlikely places.

Never Meant to Be

The greatest lesson that my healing journey has ever taught me,
is to observe but not absorb.

People will move how they move
with no regard
to how or what it does to affect you.

Some people are meant to stay exactly where they are.
Some people are meant to mess up in our lives,
to show us that their path was never meant for us
to take with them.

Someone once asked me why I keep certain parts of myself hidden. I didn't know what to say at first. But, when I think about it, after a series of events in my life, I was determined that once someone knew about all the darkness in my life, they would never look at me the same, let alone love me.

They would somehow overlook all of the light in me and only see me for my past.

Over time, I talked myself out of this. Over time, I was finally able to let people in. And in doing so, I've met some of the most amazing people in my life. And they love me just the same

...because one day, you're going to meet someone who understands that you had to go through all of that to be the person you are today.

One Day

The truth is, I was never ready for anything
I've ever had to go through or show up for.
It's always been a 'sink or swim' life for me.
But I kept showing up.
with bloodied knuckles and fought
despite the tragedy.

One day, it'll all pay off, they say.
One day, I can take off all of my armor.

They say that one day I'll meet a soul
that will be my safe harbor.

I'm just afraid I'll never believe it.

Hidden Scars

I hope you win the wars inside of your heart today,

the
ones
you
don't
tell
anyone
about.

Outgrowing The Past Versions

People only accept what they subconsciously feel like they deserve in any aspect of life.

If you've leveled up, grown, healed, or changed in any way, and people from your past no longer accept you, you have to know that it has nothing to do with you.

They don't see the vision you see now—

The goals.
The pain it took to gain that wisdom.
The pain it took to push forward.

You have done everything necessary
to move on with your life.
Whether or not they decide
to accompany you on your journey
is on them.

Just keep going.
Just keep crushing your goals.
Keep chasing your dreams.

The right people: the people
that are meant to be in your life,
they will always be there for you
without ever making you question
for a moment, where their loyalty lies.

And they will do so unconditionally.

Fool's Gold

I had to let him go. No matter how hard I tried and no matter how much love I poured into him, I couldn't save him. He didn't want to be saved. My problem is that I always see the best in people, or at least that's what I tell myself. But the truth is, I look far more closely at their potential than the person standing in front of me. I look into their eyes.

I look into the brokenness of their soul, telling myself that just because I chose to crawl out of my own darkness, somehow, I can bring them out of theirs, too. I learned the hard way that's not always the case. Sometimes, people are so content with their own chaos that they would rather bring you down with them than ever consider change or growth.

I Deserved More

I look for the depth in everything. The light, the darkness, hearts, eyes, souls. I will probably never be what you wanted me to be, and that's okay. I have endured way too much trauma in my life to ever be 'normal', but I wake up every day, and I choose to be better. I choose growth and happiness despite the pain I feel inside.

If you can't understand or love my depths when I've done nothing but love yours, you don't deserve to know mine. And I'm okay with that. I love myself enough now to be okay with being without someone who never saw the light in me. I love myself enough now to let go of anyone committed to only seeing the darkness of my past. I've evolved from that...

...and I've outgrown settling for that, too.

Rest Peacefully

The world lost
a little piece of sunshine that day,
and I lost my whole

S U N.

Manifest

Wishing on the stars is important,
Because even if no one else hears you,
your heart does.

The universe does.

Love Doesn't Fix Blind

I don't ever have to question if I loved you enough. I know I did. You know how I know? Because loving you changed me. I became a better person. I wanted to be better, but it wasn't until I learned how to let you go that I realized that it was never because of you. It was because I was always capable of it. I just didn't know it yet. I had no idea how much love I was capable of giving or how much love resided in me until I loved you.

Learning is Never-Ending

It took me years to understand that healing wasn't about being able to handle my past. I did handle it. I already got through it. Healing has been about learning to love the darkest parts of my soul and pour love into the places that haven't seen the light in a really long time.

Healing, for me, is learning to forgive others and, more importantly, forgive myself when I was lost in my self-destructive ways when I didn't know any better. And even more importantly, to learn how to love myself unconditionally. Most of the love that has been missing for the majority of my life was ironically from myself. Healing to be able to be present in the present without looking through the filters of my traumas.

Healing through the good days. Healing through the bad.
Healing and working for every single thing that I've never had.

You Created a Beast

The hardest pill for me to swallow,
out of everything that happened,
was knowing that I was always your shield
from anything that came out way,
but you were never mine.

I can count more times of you being against me than beside me.
I can close my eyes and still feel your rage,
as you mistook me for the enemy;
when all I was trying to do was save you.

All I was trying to do was love you.
Regardless of how much it hurt to watch it all unfold,
you can't ever say that I wasn't solid.
You can't ever say that I didn't stand beside you,
ready to go to war
because I was; I was there through all of it.

I can rest knowing that I did my best.
I can heal and let go,
knowing it wasn't because I didn't want it.

I would've never given up.
I would've never walked away.
My love for you was so pure.

The woman you see standing before you
is a little different now.
You taught me how to fight through the darkness.
You leaving, taught me how to become my own light.

My Drug

He created this hollowness inside of me,
deeper than I could ever explain
and the only thing that filled that void
was him.

He. Was. My. Drug.

He was killing me,
and I just kept going back for more.

Just one more kiss.
Just one more hit.
Just one more night.

Loving him was like dancing with the devil,
just to feel alive.

Ghosts Reside Within

Most of our pain resides in the ghosts of people and periods of our lives that echo throughout our lives.

Most of our hearts are lost to the ones who never stayed.

Pieces of you with them.
Pieces of them with you.

I feel like if we didn't have anything lingering,
for the most part, we'd all be alright

It's the hauntings that remain,
that torture us;
be it consciously or subconsciously.

These are the tragedies that shape us.

There's pain that either breaks us or gives us drive,
and it's okay to do both.

In my journey, I've learned the only way to get past it,
is to acknowledge it completely.

We must learn exactly where and how deep the roots of these thorns go, before we can ever plan for their extraction, for complete healing.

We have to dig down and go deep.
We have to find where our ghosts are dwelling.

Then, we have to learn how to let them go.

Strangers Again

And just like that,
they became strangers again.

Strangers with memories,
strangers with love,
strangers with pain
and the connection between them
was lost forever.

Nothing more than a flash
and a temporary moment of him and I.
Merely an echo
and a blink of existence, in time.

/Au Revoir/

It took me years to get here.
It took years to accept everything that happened
and learn to let go.
But I can sit here and say with a straight face,
I'm honestly at peace with the way everything happened.
I wouldn't have grown into the person that is standing before you today.

I laugh a little harder, cry with purpose, and love more purely.

I was able to learn the value of each moment as I saw that time goes faster than any of us could ever anticipate.

It took trauma and tragedy,
but I'm finally awake now.
I see life differently now—better.

I became a better person from all of it.

It Felt Like A Dream

I don't have answers as to why anything
happened between us the way it did
but it didn't make it any less real.

Ocean Souls

If you only knew the tragedy
in the souls of those
who find peace
in chaos.

Lessons

When you learn that everything people choose to do and how they choose to react to any situation is a choice, life becomes so much simpler.

It becomes so much easier to accept.

They chose to hurt you. They chose to put you down. Those are the things that they chose to do. There are no excuses for people who inflict pain on purpose.

That is all of the closure that you need, babe.

Grace and mercy and love and understanding all exist, and those are not character traits that they hold inside.

You deserve so much more than that, and I hope that it doesn't take you as long as it took me to learn that.

Thorns

There seems to be a misunderstanding.
You do not have to like my thorns.
My thorns are there to protect ME.
They were grown from the stems around my heart
to protect the delicate flower in my soul

from

people

like

you.

I Believe In You

I have no doubts that you are
going to come out of this
on the other side,
stronger than before.

Just like the seasons,
everything that passes,
also brings new life with time.

I See You Fighting

Look at you,
breaking toxic cycles, family curses,
and the chains
from the trauma of the past.

Look at you,
putting a smile on your face
and never giving up,
knowing the bad days

NEVER LAST.

Angels in Human Form

My favorite gifts from the universe are finding people who live among the same frequencies that my soul does. People on the same mission. People with the same fire. The same fight.

There's no awkward conversations. There's no misunderstandings. You're both here for the same purpose: to bring the same messages to the world. To shine light in areas of darkness that only the brave souls venture through. For no other reason than to let people stuck in it know they are not alone. All to blaze a trail for every person that comes after you so they can find their way out.

The connection doesn't have to be romantic, and even if it is, it doesn't have to be a forever thing. You both walk with this understanding of what your purposes are as friends, as lovers, as acquaintances. Your paths were destined to cross.

Your messages need to be heard and found, with the understanding that we have to save as many people as we can because there was a time when we almost didn’t make it out of the wars in our own minds.

This is why writers become friends
Suicide survivors become mental health advocates
Recovering addicts become counselors.

We carry a message of hope for everyone that follows after. Not everyone can do it, but for those of us who can and who choose to, we do it until our last breath.

For the hope that if we can save even ONE life, it would all be worth it.

We've survived the fires.
We came out of the darkness.
We're acquainted with it.
We know our way in and out of it.

And when you come across people who carry the same torches in the dark that you do, you create so much more than hope.
You create love for life.
You create healing.
You create change together.

And there is nothing more beautiful than that.
There is nothing purer than that.

Angels among the masses,
covered in battle scars with hearts of gold.

Silence

We always hear of the silence that comes with pain. The pain that is so deep we turn numb, cold, and expressionless about it.

I never understood the sentiment and silent pain until these last few years, when my world fell apart, and the world kept turning. It's a feeling that is hard to describe in any other words, *but the noise on the inside becomes louder than the noise around you, and you just become silent.*

Like pain that pierces through your heart so deep, all you can do is focus on breathing through it.

The walls feel like they're closing in. The sun doesn't seem to shine as bright some days, and on other days, we find ourselves avoiding it.

The deafening silence night is suddenly something we can relate to and strangely becomes our comfort through it.

Pain comes in many forms. The forms that drop you to your knees. The forms that have you in tears at the very thought of it. The form that makes you become hyper-independent to prevent any further letdown in your life.

The pain that you can smile through. The pain that gives you drive and ambition. And last but not least, the pain that makes you silent. The pain feels like broken ribs because absolutely no one around you can see it, but you feel it with every breath.

I haven't quite figured out how to navigate through getting past this part yet, but I can tell you that it is real—my God, is it real. And as maddening as the silence is, it also feels safe: no chaos around me, even if there is chaos within me.
It's safe—even if it hurts.

At this point, I've accepted being able to tolerate hurting myself with mere memories of the past rather than putting myself through the thought of anyone in my external world creating new emotional or physical wounds.

Until I can learn to trust that not everyone around me is a monster, I stay silent. I observe. I create my own safe places internally to learn where I need to heal first.

And the first step of that has been learning to shield what pieces I have left in my heart.

Pieces

There are always missing pieces.
Missing pieces that you find
yourself yearning for.

Healing doesn't make these disappear;
on the contrary,
I suppose it places all the empty holes on display.
Not to torment us,
but as a way to show us:
'This is where we need to heal first.'

Eternity Echoes

Despite all of the heartache,
I still got to feel your love.
Even if I didn't get to have it
until the very end.

Hearts That Bleed Black

If you ask him to describe her heart,
he'll tell you that it is beautiful melancholy...

...but the kind that makes you fall in love with the dark.

"Dimittere" Letting Go

We have to let go sometimes. Be it people, places, or things. It's a part of life that no one really tells us about. It's one of the things that we have to figure out on our own.

We must learn to let go, no matter how much it hurts. No matter how much we poured into it. No matter how much you love them.

Somehow, at some point in my life, I had convinced myself that having half-love was better than having no love at all. I had convinced myself that having someone to wipe my tears away, even if they caused them, was better than not having anyone to do so.

That was the unhealed version of myself talking. I know better now. I know I deserve better now.

I know now that no matter how much you love someone when you respect yourself and learn to love yourself, you'll learn how to give that same love that you seek to yourself. You learn how to let go of people and situations that only cause more pain. And you'll also be able to recognize it.

I've learned that letting something go once and being sad for a while is better than dealing with the **continuous emotional trauma** that comes with being with someone who does not respect you or care about inflicting wounds upon you--in any way.

I've found more peace in letting go than I ever did holding on. It's become a breath of fresh air. It's realizing the cup of love that I was drinking from wasn't love at all.

It's recognizing the poison and what was making me sick, metaphorically, and refusing to be anywhere near it now.

It's thanking the universe for the lessons but also learning how to breathe on your own again.

It's learning that it's okay to acknowledge everything you went through to process it and learn from it but trusting the process so you learn how not to let your emotions consume you. Grief is real. Separation anxiety and trauma are real. Abandonment trauma is real. You have to dig deep down to where you feel the sting of the loss the most. Dig down and pinpoint the roots. And then heal there first. Love there first. Pour into that part of yourself first.

I swear everything else falls into place after that, but you have to first acknowledge it, Then you have to allow yourself to feel it, and Then you have to grieve it. And then learn how to love it. Even the most broken parts of it.

We have to let go sometimes to save what's left inside. We have to keep going despite any pain internally that we hide.

We have to let go sometimes because we have to make room for better things to come. We have to hold on to hope in fear of what our hearts might become.

We have to let go, sometimes, because if it was meant to be any other way, it would be. We have to learn from the pain despite all of the tragedy.

We have to let go to blaze the trail for the rest. We have to let go, even when letting go becomes our heart's biggest test.

Cold Fall Winds

How poetic that somehow the cold fall winds will forever remind me of you. Of the day you left. The winds of change swirling around us, at the same time that your destructive winds shredded everything of which we were at the same time.

Unseen. Cold. Destructive. The metaphor around me telling me that all things must end.

The beauty of the leaves changing colors and the trees reminding us how important it is to let go.

The way the leaves dance in the wind, even as it is their end.

How poetic it all turned out to be. Us. The winds. The seasons. I found peace in letting go, just as the trees do.

But I'm sure they weep just the same as me.

Hope

They say all good things come to an end.
And even though it may seem like a dark statement,
I see hope in it.
Because there's always a balance between life, and the universe;
the yin and the yang to everything.

If good things must end,
then that also means
all bad things eventually do too.

I Want a Protector

I used to think that the only person who could ever understand me was someone who also had similar pain. There really is an unexplained level of understanding between trauma survivors. But as time came and went, and I met people with demons that matched my own, the more I realized it really had nothing to do with it at all. Even more so, with the more I began to heal myself.

There were some individuals who, despite having been through similar things that I have, had no desire to heal themselves or become better. Some people really are perfectly content in their own chaos. No remorse for who takes the wrath of the flames around them. With the same response to everyone saying, 'That's just who I am.'

Let me tell you something. Despite anything, and I mean anything, that I've been through in my life, I make it a point to learn my lessons so that I don't carry that trauma onto the next person who enters my life.

I chose to be better and grow every time.

It is a **CHOICE**.

Do not let anyone tell you otherwise, and at the end of the day, whether or not the person standing in front of me had similar scars to mine or not, I'm going based on what version they bring to me after.

Is the person in front of me willing to be open and honest, and protect, not just me, but my heart as well?

Not only from the world, but also from themselves?

At this point, I don't care if he's more angel or more devil. I just want someone who could never imagine causing an ounce of pain towards me.

To look at me with the same wonder I look at them with. Whether we're holding hands in the heavens or marching together down to hell, I want a warrior.

Someone who won't hesitate.

Someone who sees the wars in my eyes
as a place to show **M E R C Y**,
and not as a threat.

Things No One Told Me

No one talks about the part of healing where you heal too much, and you have trouble connecting with anyone else after, who hasn't also healed their trauma.

There is nothing appealing about anything temporary once you learn to love yourself.

Your circle gets smaller.
You wake up and realize that over time, without even knowing it, you've become someone new.

You mourn the person that you used to be,
but you lay them to rest gracefully.

The hardest part of all of it , is learning that you can't make anyone see you the way that you see yourself.

Healed or unhealed.
You have to move forward with accepting that people create their own perceptions, and the only one you are responsible for, here forward, *is your own.*

The Wolf In Me

It's ironic, in a way,
how I have always referred to my spirit as a wolf.

It's almost a coincidence,
how I loved and admired you
the same way that I admired the moon.

Maybe we always were meant to be
that love story between the wolf and the moon.

Always apart.
Never within reach.
Crying out on lonely nights.
Always in sight,
but no possible way you could ever be mine.

Not really, anyway.

Maybe this was always our destiny.
Maybe you'll always be my moon.
Maybe I'll always be the wolf.

Trauma Sessions

My therapist asked me one day what happiness looked like for me. I couldn't pinpoint it at first. I'd never been asked that before. What would a happy life actually look like? What was the one thing I had always looked for? Yearned for? I came from nothing, so it was never materialistic.

I closed my eyes for a minute and then responded to her that, to me, a happy life looks like peace. It's the feeling of being safe.

The two things being birthed into chaos that I've never really had. The things that I've never really seen up close. That's what I imagine a happy life to be. Without struggle. Without worry of the person beside you being a ticking time bomb at any given moment.

I want a life where I don't have to watch the body language and tones of every person around me and do not have to be hyper-aware of all of my surroundings at all times.

I will call myself happy when I can find arms that won't necessarily calm my internal storms but protect me from the storms of everything going on around me.

Just long enough to take off my armor,

even if just for a minute.

I can't begin to tell you how heavy it all is to carry armor like that (and for as long as I can remember too).

I was almost convinced that I was never going to be able to take it off. If not even for anyone else but myself.

To give my soul a rest for a while from being strong for so long.

From being on fight or flight for all of my life.

She just listens; she's not even writing anything at this point. She lets me talk. Looking at the storms of memories crashing in and out of my eyes, I talk about what a safe life would feel like for me.

She places her hand on mine and tells me to come back.
She tells me to breathe.
She tells me that even though I still battle the wounds of my traumas within, that I'm not going through any of it in present time anymore.

I take a deep breath, and she tells me I'm doing great.
Then, as I was about to break, she lifted my head up and told me, *"There is a balance to everything in life. If you exist, and the way that you love exists, you have to know that it exists out there in other people too. There are people who feel just as scared and alone as you do. There are people who have never even been through a quarter of what you have, but they also carry such love within. There are good people everywhere. You exist. You are proof of that. If you ever feel like you're doubting other people's intentions because of your broken trust, just remember that* ***'YOU EXIST'****; so therefore, your counterpart will exist as well. You have to remember that even though there is evil in this world, evil is not behind every set of eyes you meet. I know even more than your heart being broken, you have had your trust broken repeatedly for a lifetime, and it's normal for you to be afraid. But good people exist. I feel like you just needed to be reminded of that."*

And she didn't know exactly how much I needed to hear that, but maybe she did.

When your trust is broken, it takes a little longer to heal from that. It takes a world of effort to drop your walls down to let anyone close enough to hurt you again and even more so to let someone love you.

But living in boxes was never the life meant for the human heart. We are meant to learn. We are meant to feel. We are meant to grow. Aristotle even said we don't learn without pain.

It's all a part of the process.

So, if you're at a point where you feel like you can't let anyone close, I just want to remind you what my therapist reminded me.

YOU EXIST. So therefore, your counterpart is out there and exists too.

You'll never know it or find it if you don't drop your walls down to the beauty of possibilities of good with new beginnings.

You only learn if you try.

I know someone else out there needs to hear that too.

Numb Yourself

There's a fine line between
pushing through the pain,
and distracting yourself from it,

I hope you never
have to learn that the hard way
like I did.

My Bittersweet Reality

The most crucial and pinnacle
moment in my healing,
was coming to the realization
that the person I fell in love with
and the person standing in front of me,
were two completely *different* people.

Hope In The Damned

I think that's why dark stories
always gave me so much comfort.

A place in existence
where even if it was fiction,
even the worst of humanity
knew the purest forms of love.

There are tales of beauties falling for beasts
since the beginning of time.
Tales of villains burning down the world
together with their mates by their side.

Loyalty, even in the darkest of places.

That sense of love
for even the most broken of us
has always given me hope.

Where the world saw
darkness and brokenness inside,
they don't.
The ones who love the unlovable,
how poetic.

These are the tales that told us
that there was someone out there meant for all of us.

I believed that kind of bond was real
until I didn't anymore.
I believed it so goddamn hard,
because that's how much I loved you.

—but maybe that's all they are, just stories.

You'll Find Me

Despite all of the places that are beautiful
and full of sunshine in this world,
you'll find me in the dark.

Where the moon guides us,
where the candles burn bright,
and where the twilight creatures roam.

You'll find me where the stars shine at night
and where the wolves welcome you home.

I Used To Miss The Old Me

I used to miss the old me. The little one with wonderous dreams. The one who danced under the moon and wasn't afraid of anything.

I used to miss the old me, but she had so much to learn. Naïve with a narrow vision, with so much wisdom still left to *earn.*

I used to miss the old me and all that she used to be Before every loss, heartbreak, and unspoken tragedy.

I used to miss the old me, back when I used to follow the butterflies and the birds. Chasing my heart and wishing on stars, but she had a voice that could never be heard.

I used to miss the old me until I fell in love with this version of myself. Heart on my sleeve, eyes wide open, and a special knowledge gained from surviving hell.

I used to miss the old me, but I had so much to grow. The person that I've become has endured so much more than I can ever show.

I used to miss the old me, but I know I had to endure it to get here today. Life has taken everything from me but also put something new in its place.

I used to miss the old me, and I'm sure some of you do too. How beautifully tragic it is to fall in love with ourselves as we become someone new.

I used to miss the old me, but I love her just the same. I'm just a completely different person now who walks around with the same name.

More Than Meets The Eyes

Those of us who survive hell speak a language and see life through different eyes than most.

Life humbled us young. We had to learn how to heal ourselves because no one came to save us like the stories told. It takes a very special person to see into the softness and love that we hold deep within our eyes, behind the flames of our past.

You just have to be brave enough to let us get close. You just have to be patient and show us that we are safe with you.

And I swear to God, we'll break the walls down ourselves; we'll come running out with our arms wide open, tears running down our faces, and show you a love deeper than anything you have ever known. We're more than our trauma. We're more than our pain.

It Was Always The Hope

It was always the hope. The hope that you'll wake up one day and realize that everything that happened was a mistake. The hope that one day you'd wake up and realize that it was always my hand you were supposed to be holding. It was the hope that you'd wake up and realize exactly how much I loved you and see everything I did for you even after you chose someone else.

It was the hope that you never could look at anyone else the way that you looked at me. It was the hope that you would come back and be the man that I always knew you could be. The man you promised to be. It was the hope that your heart ached for mine the same way that mine did for yours after all this time. It was the hope that we really could overcome everything we went through. And after all of that, at the end of the day, you would always choose me. The way that it was always you, for me.

It was the hope that we could go out and do everything in this world that we said we would do together. It was the hope of having the family life that we both deserved, the life that neither of us got to experience growing up. It was the hope that you would be by my side as we grew old. It was the hope that we'd make it. Despite all of the bullshit, I still hoped that we would make it.

And in the end, to this day, it's the hope that hurts the most. Because every day that's passed, not a single one of those things has happened or come close. Illusions and pretty words of you telling me everything I wanted to hear but never meaning it. Saying you miss me but still choosing a life without me. Saying just enough to keep me holding on but never enough to be the man you were supposed to be. The toxic cycle of not loving me right and also never fully letting me go.

The silent ache of the remnants of what my heart was before you broke it. The echoes of laughter and what I thought was love in all of the moments we shared. Ever fading and being lost to time each day that passes.

Nothing more than a memory. Memories that I've learned to allow to fade because remembering anything hurts too much to reach back anymore.

As of late, though, I've shifted the hope from 'you' to myself.

I hope that my heart can recover from this one day. I hope that I can wake up and say that I'm okay and finally mean it.

I hope that the pain subsides with time.

I hope that I continue to become everything I was meant to be in this life without you.

I hope that I can still chase every dream and smile, knowing that I made it.

Knowing that it means just the same, and the moments aren't anything less to experience just because of your absence.

I hope that I can fully mourn your loss so I can properly let you go enough to learn to move on and let go in a healthy way.

I hope that my heart remains beautiful despite the destruction and chaos you left behind within it. I hope flowers grow over the scars in my soul so that they are no longer recognizable in the future.

I hope that I can look back and smile, knowing that word (hope) is the only thing that pulled me through **ALL OF IT**.

Never Again

I'm done trying to change who I am for any reason--for any person. What I will change is my perception. My priorities. My boundaries. The way I care for myself and others. My reactions to situations that I cannot control.

I will change the coldness in my heart created from past pain. I will change my goals. I will allow my dreams to be limitless.

I will change everything else I can to make this life beautiful.

But I will never change my soul.

It's Time

This isn't your burial.
You've merely been planted.

It's time to bloom, my darling.

Always

It will always be the ones
you never see coming
that change your life.

For better or for worse.

Learning and Growing Without You

I’ve learned how to grow gardens in the pieces of me that died.

I learned how to create light from within when I'm surrounded by nothing but darkness around me.

I’ve learned how to swim in the deepest seas of sorrow that I’ve encountered.

I learned how to write my pain away and let my pen bleed ink for me.

I've learned how to use my voice to help heal others and be a guiding light in a world that makes people feel alone.

I’m not the same broken girl you left all those years ago.

I’ve learned how to teach others to fight and extend learning how to become a beacon of hope.

Time Heals

It'll come in phases.
There will be days when you feel like
you can take on the world.

Other days it will feel like the weight of the world
is crushing your ability to breathe

Both days will come.
Both days are crucial.
Both days are necessary.
Both days are a part of the healing journey
that no one really tells you about.

It's important to teach yourself
to take everything one day at a time.
Sometimes, even one hour at a time.
One breath at a time.

The Wise Ones

The naïve will tell you to master your fears, and you'll find peace.

What they don't tell you is once you've mastered every fear and doubt, you only have one thing left to deal with time.

The wise will always tell you there's never enough time.

Unconditional Love

I would've done so much more
than destroy the world
to prove my love for you

I would've destroyed myself.
And that, by far, is what scares me the most
about how hard I love.

Denial

That's not a dark angel babe,
that's a demon.
But I know how stubborn
your heart is.
You still have to see it
to believe it.

Camouflage

It was all a façade.
A mask.
A cry for help.
Anything to find a way
to numb the pain.

Camouflage smiles and working myself
until I became numb,
to distract my heart
from feeling pain like that ever

AGAIN.

The Bigger Picture

I've lost so much in my short years.
I've lost friends, lovers, hope,
And everything in between.

Each phase I went through
demanded a piece of me to be left behind.

No matter how much I tried to fight it
or how many times I tried to press rewind.

Trying to hold on, trying to let go.
Life is so ever-changing, like a River.

Healing has been more teaching myself to not resist,
and gracefully learn to go with the flow.

Reality

Life has a funny way of making us grow.
It will humble you
faster than you could ever anticipate or even know.
It will give you everything you want
and just as fast, take it all away.
Just to teach you a lesson,
that you need to carry with you,
to turn the page.

Accountability

The hardest pill for me to ever swallow was accepting that I played a part in a lot of what I went through. I was a part of the blame for how bad things got. I was a part of the reason why I was in it for so long.

It was learning to forgive the ugliest parts of my personality that came out while I was in fight or flight. It was accepting that I carried both darkness in my soul, and light.

It was accepting that I still had so much to learn, even at a time when I was convinced I knew it all. I had to teach myself to stand back up after every mistake and fall.

Closure

I never got official closure from him like I thought I needed. It came to me in pieces.

It came on the mornings when I was able to watch a sunrise without having my day ruined before 8 am. It came on the holidays I was able to enjoy with family and friends, who reminded me what laughter felt like again.

It came on the days I realized that letting go did less damage than holding onto that rope. It came on the days right after I felt like there could never be hope.

It came on the nights when I realized that I was safer alone. It came with the moments I realized I didn't need him by my side to grow.

Never Again

I never want to be that girl that pretends she doesn't feel anything ever again. I feel deeply. I love even harder. I'll never water myself down again. The only heart that deserves mine is the one that sees me fully and loves me for all of the depths that I carry in every inch of my soul.

You. Always.

Life was never meant to be easy.
It was always you
who was meant to be

STRONG.

Beautiful Fragments

When I say, 'He broke me beautifully,'
Understand this:
I am not glorifying what he did to me.
What I endured was atrocious.
However, who I became after the destruction
has been nothing short of beautiful.

That kind of growth can only be inspired by soul-shattering pain.

Life is always reminding us,
that sunshine always comes after rain.

Burning Bridges

The most beautiful part of the healing journey is with every phase we go through and grow through, we break ties with old versions of ourselves.

There's always pieces that we'll miss, pieces we weren't ready to let go of

But all of the pieces that led to our self-destructive ways, all the pieces that were naïve, all the pieces that served us no good, those pieces fall off too.

Watching that part happen and watching a new part of yourself be born, it's so liberating.

It's so healing.

Your eyes open again.

Your life changes for the better eventually as you learn new things and learn new ways to handle things that are thrown your way.

The moment of realization after the transformation. There's nothing more beautiful than that.

Hold on.

You're almost there too; I can see it.

Dark nights don't last forever. Every cocoon will open. Rainbows always come after the storms.

The sun will come out again. And she'll smile, looking back at you, waiting to bring you back into her light.

Changing Perception

Training your mind to be on your side is crucial in any part of healing, merely for the fact that our minds are typically our nemesis after trauma.

We can have every aspect of our lives together or 'fixed' after tragedy, but our hearts are always the last ones to get the message.

They're always the last ones to accept that they're safe now. To allow love to come through any walls. To learn to trust again.

Retraining our minds is the hardest but the most important step of our journey.

You have to tell yourself over and over again until you believe it. Positive attitude and thinking seem almost impossible at times, but we have to fake it til' we make it when it comes to that aspect of it.

Eventually it all goes from being a thought, to being an action, to being a way of life. It'll never happen if we don't start somewhere, though, right?

One thought at a time. One step at a time. One day at a time. And then one day, you'll wake up and see:

It's not just a thought anymore; it will become your new reality.

Hope That It's Real

Do you want to know what I hate about this generation? We've somehow managed to kill love. We merely hold on to an idea of it but somehow fail to keep it. We fail to embody it. We failed to embrace it. We fail to find it. It's become nothing short of a false hope. Nothing short of a facade.

We pour so much of ourselves into broken people because we, too, know what it feels like to be starved of love. Only to have more pieces of our souls ripped from us, stolen, and stepped on. Tossed aside like it's no big deal. Connections fall dead for no reason. Forgetting the pieces that they put of themselves into those people. For getting the moments shared. The feelings felt. Forgetting the person standing in front of them carries a heart too, that was vulnerable and hurt because of the promises that came out of their mouths. So reckless. So heartless. So broken. All of us.

Actions that show the exact opposite. Creating this endless circle of distress. This endless circle of pain. I'd give anything in the world to meet someone who can see the value of what comes with loving someone who has a heart bigger than the oceans, without taking advantage or hurting them.

I've never seen it. I've never felt it.

Like the winds, it's become unpredictable, invisible, and unreachable. Felt but not seen and gone just as fast as it comes.

Never standing still. Never within our reach. We're left wandering this life with bleeding hearts, period. Loving the ghosts of our past because it's all we have...

...a million memories
and an idea of what love should be, but it isn't.

Look At You Now

There's something so surreal about the feeling and the vulnerability it takes to allow someone to truly see your heart. The courage it takes to let someone feel it. The ability to drop down those walls that were necessary at one point to let love in again.

To learn how to trust again, because life showed you everything that happened in your life that was for a reason. It doesn't mean that you weren't meant for love. It doesn't mean you'll never experience complete happiness. It just meant that your time wasn't back then. It wasn't with that person. You had to heal the first period. You had to become receptive to something better, and here you are, standing at the bravery of a new beginning, remembering what it's like to feel alive again.

And I've never seen you look so beautiful.

My Best Quality

Loving hard is my character trait.
I'll never let the pain of my past
ruin that for me in the future.

I always come in with the best intentions.
I always come in solid.
How we end from there is on

YOU.

It's Not Your Fault

Just like you can't see other people's intentions,
you can't make them see yours either.

No matter how good.

No matter how pure.

You can't love them harder to make them see you.
They have to see it and want it for themselves.

Expecting anything outside of that only causes heartbreak.

Protect Your Heart

Be wary of who you
open up your soul to.
From experience,
people with ill intentions
will use it as a road map
to learn exactly what your
weaknesses are to hurt you.

Mirror or Glass View?

All of the wise people say,
'Only a monster can love a monster.'

And I sit here every night and ask myself,
"Did that make me a monster
for loving Y O U?"

The Journey

It was a long way back up. I fell down more times than I could count. I tried giving up more times than I'd like to admit. I numbed myself to survive for so long. Until one day, I sat in the midst of all the chaos in my life and watched it all flash before my eyes like a movie.

I had an epiphany. I was the source of all of my pain, but I was also my own solution.

I had everything inside of me that I needed to pull myself out of this mess that I called life. I started small. I started with just waking up and changing my mindset. Be better. Be positive. Be optimistic, even if there's no reason to.

I told myself, 'Let's do this internally first'. As expected, life kept throwing punches, but the way I was taking the hits became different.

I started to notice that I wasn't controlled by my emotions anymore. After that, I worked on what emotion was triggered, when it happened. It was also learning to let go of the things that triggered me in the first place.

'Heal this part first,' I told myself. Then, before I knew it, I looked in the mirror, and I didn't see a hopeless woman anymore. I saw the same girl with hunger in her eyes that I had when I was a child all over again. I hadn't seen her in so long that I forgot how beautiful she was. Finally craving better. Finally craving more.

That craving turned into a drive with time. It was the pain and heartbreak that fueled my passion for life again. It took me time to learn how to use that for a positive instead of a negative. And then, before I knew it, The chains from my past broke off as my energy started to shift and vibrate higher.

I became unstoppable.

I had to dwell in the darkest parts of my soul for some time before I was able to adjust my vision through it to look for the light and find my way out of it. Carrying a torch with me the whole way out, guiding the other lost souls along with me.

We'll all make it out of this. We have to. Someone has to survive these stories to blaze a path for everyone else.

Someone has to make it out of this alive.

And there's no way in hell that I go down without fighting and doing so with everything I got. It's finally time to fight for good. It's time to fight for what I want, for something better—to get out of the darkness that I called love and life for so long; it's time to become the light and live life the way that we were always supposed to, but forgot how to for so long.

Paradox

What you have to understand about me is the depth of my love carries equal amounts of pain.
My successes carry double the amount of failures. My happy days carry ten times more sad days.

You only see my glow, not the depths underneath it.
Yes, I carry light now. I own it.
But it also carries just as much deep, pain-ridden darkness.

Hidden away and broken.
Bleeding from the inside out.
Using my own bloodshed to help heal others in similar pain.

There's no secret to surviving, just keep breathing.
Just keep shining your light.

Your inner luminous heart will light the way;
you just have to trust it.
But you'll see the light shows you the way, but it doesn't stop the wounds from piercing your soul.

You have to dig deep down in there yourself
and rip them out from the source.

And in case no one told you, it's not a bloodless act. It's ripping apart the very essence of every ounce of who you were before.

It's patching up and cleaning up the mess after.
It's sleepless nights.
And it's never giving up.
It's fighting every day.

One. Day. At. A. Time.

If It's Heavy, Let It Go

The pain hit different when you opened up your soul to them, showing them the road map to every bleeding wound in your heart.

All we wanted was to be understood, to be loved correctly, the way that every person failed before.

And the only thing they did was look for a new empty space in your heart to create a new wound and then leave Instead of protecting you from pain the way that they said they would.

Promises mean nothing to me now. I trust even less. The time robs us of everything and leaves us to clean up the mess.

Keep Growing

Some people focus so hard on who you used to be
that they miss out on the person you're becoming.

Rest assured, it's their loss, babe.

Not everyone is meant to go to the top with you.
They'll all sort themselves out eventually.

No one knows how far you've come.
No one knows how hard you've fought,
but I do. I see you.
And I am so fucking proud of you.

Just keep going.
You've come too far to go back now.
You've come too far to give up now.

Fickle Love

Everyone is just walking around
destroying each other
past the point of return.

Putting a rose on it,
calling it love,
then watching as it all

B U R N S.

Patiently Waiting

I can't wait for the day
that I can finally put your
memory to rest
in my heart.

Denial Will Cost You

It was hard for me, you know?
Harder than I thought.

I had to accept that the source of my happiness
had also turned into the source of my pain.

Something changes inside of you when that happens
and acknowledging that hurt more
than I can ever put into words.

It's Enough For Me

They say, according to quantum physics, the sound of our voices can vibrate to the edge of the universe, right?

And according to the multiverse theory, somewhere out there lies another dimension where we exist.

It has to be why your voice still holds so much power over me. It must still be my home and both another space and time.

I can let go and find peace in knowing that somewhere out there, I'm still yours, and you're still mine.

It's Yours Forever

My darkest nights weren't overcome by searching for the sun. Some days, it never came.

My worst days were survived by learning how to navigate in those dark waters and learning how to become my own light when I was lost.

And let me tell you a secret. Once you figure that out, no one can ever steal it from you again. It wasn't given. It was earned. And it's **YOURS**. It's yours to use to navigate through anything your soul ventures through after.

It Has To Be Out There

Yes, I'm aware of the potential pain that comes with opening up
and loving someone new again,
but maybe I'm just a different breed.

I can't think of a better way to live.
I can't think of a better way to die.
It's always been worth the risk for me.

So, trust me when I say,
that love is my most elaborate form of self-destruction.

Because I mean it.

Because I'll always choose it.

And I'll never stop looking until I find it.

You Were My World

When they asked me how it was possible to love you the way I did when we endured so much darkness

I told them, 'Because no matter how dark the skies became, I looked at you, and I still saw the stars'.

It just took more time than I thought to learn to love myself the same way enough to let you go afterward.

Lust

Loving someone like you
was always a war.
A war that left me bloodthirsty,
always wanting more.

Dimmitas

Take the memories with you when you leave,
they serve no purpose anymore
other than bringing pain.

Soul Deep

I wish I was the kind of person that didn't let things other people told me affect me. I wish I didn't feel everything so deeply sometimes. I wish that I could just let everything roll off of my back. I wish I could let every harsh word float off into the universe somewhere else, anywhere else but directly to my soul: the place where every gut-wrenching, horrific word, every knife in my back, every action against me, all tally on my heart. Marking it, as if it's keeping count; like keeping count is going to help by remembering every betrayal in my life.

It doesn't help, and I didn't choose it.
It's the one thing I dislike about my heart.
It's something that takes a toll on my spirit.

There is no in-between for people like me. I either feel everything, literally everything, or I feel absolutely nothing. And I still haven't decided which version is worse.

I Know Better Now

Somewhere along the line
I became so accustomed to being let down,
that I confused the bare minimum
as *effort.*

Beauty In Darkness

All I want to be remembered as
is the girl who always found
beauty in darkness
and as the girl who taught others how to find it too.

No Matter What

Happily ever after to me
never meant perfect.

Happily ever after to me,
means even on the worst days,
even on the darkest nights,
even on the nights we can't agree
we'll always choose each other.

For the rest of our days...

...and I can only hope to taste that in this life.

About the Author

Brianna Terese Vigil, also known in the writing and poetry world as B. Vigil, is a dark poetry author from Albuquerque, New Mexico, USA. She started writing as a teenager, which continues as her journey now as an adult. She was published in her debut book, Beauty In Darkness. She has also been published in the previous anthologies: As Darkness Falls, Don't Forget Him, A Touch of Temptation, Love Is Helpless, Silent Tears of a Woman, UKRAINE: The Night and the Fire, and Shadow of the Soul. >

Brianna is a small town girl who writes on the beauty in life. Be it from darkness, love, pain, and now healing. She reminds us that there is always something to see even in the worst of times, and she allows her readers to remember it's ok to not be ok all the time. And with her new book, Brianna now shows us that it's even more beautiful to heal amongst the chaos after. Leaving a roadmap and blazing a trail for all of the broken-hearted people, with wild dreams like her

Brianna also works in the hospitals as a Registered Respiratory Therapist by night, saving people with not only her words, but also with her hands too. Her only goal to save as many people as she can, in her time here with us.

You can find all of Brianna's writing on all social media platforms under the hashtags #bvigil or #bvigilauthor and her direct link to her website with all of her books and information is:

https://linktr.ee/B.vigil_author

Printed in Great Britain
by Amazon

41573306R00079